BROKEN
to
Beautiful

Healing After Sexual Abuse

Marcia White

WESTBOW
PRESS®
A DIVISION OF THOMAS NELSON
& ZONDERVAN

WestBow Press books may be ordered through booksellers or by contacting:

WestBow Press
A Division of Thomas Nelson & Zondervan
1663 Liberty Drive
Bloomington, IN 47403
www.westbowpress.com
1 (866) 928-1240

ISBN: 978-1-9736-0599-7 (sc)
ISBN: 978-1-9736-0600-0 (hc)
ISBN: 978-1-9736-0598-0 (e)

Library of Congress Control Number: 2017916612

Print information available on the last page.

WestBow Press rev. date: 11/14/2017

Contents

My Story

Your Healing and Future

My Story

Chapter 1
Great Beginnings

E ARLY ONE SPRING MORNING, in the hustling and bustling city of Baltimore, Maryland—after a very prolonged labor—I finally made my grand entrance into the world. I arrived on the scene with glistening black hair, deep brown eyes, a glowing olive complexion, and a shrill scream that awakened the entire nursery. I instantly became the newest princess in our growing family. I was "daughter number three," as my dad still affectionately calls me. My reign as princess did not last long; within two years I was succeeded by daughter number four. What a blessed family we were!

Our family resided in Brooklyn, a Baltimore neighborhood, during the early years of my life. I do not have many memories of living there; however, my fondest recollections of Brooklyn all center on summer.

Marcia White

Our close-knit family of six rented a small apartment in the city. The streets were noisy, day and night, as the traffic whizzed by continuously. The constant echo of sirens and horns, along with the sultry air, made it almost impossible to fall asleep at night. As the bright sun rose each morning, we were certain that it would be another scorching day.

Mom would often take us outdoors to catch a cool breeze. The tiny fenced yard did not allow much space for adventure, but it did let us view what was happening in the neighborhood. Our favorite sound was the jolly music that reverberated as the ice cream truck approached our crowded street. The neighborhood would immediately look like a colony of ants as children ran to get money and then got in line at the brightly adorned truck. The banana, coconut, and fudge popsicles were delicious; however, my personal favorite was the icy snow cone. With wide eyes, I would watch as the ice cream man smothered the shaved ice with blueberry syrup and then topped it with warm marshmallow cream. I can still taste the creamy goodness today!

Life was good in our small apartment on Jack Street; however, our parents wanted to raise us in the country. They began making plans for their desire to become a reality, so when I was four years old, Mom and Dad announced that we would soon be relocating to West Virginia. This move would allow us to be closer to our family and to make many new friends. I remember the excitement over the opportunity to live around my grandparents and our many cousins. The best part of the news was that Dad was purchasing the house beside my grandparents' home. Shortly after the announcement, we moved into a "holler" in beautiful, mountainous West Virginia. What a welcome change it was from the busy city of Baltimore. Much of our sizable extended family already lived in the holler. With each of our cousins and some other neighborhood playmates, there was always a new adventure as the sun arose each morning. There were woods to explore, trees to climb, gardens to work, farm animals to feed, and cold spring water to drink. Living in the country allowed us many chances to enjoy the great outdoors.

My sisters and I were very content with life in our new home in West Virginia. My parents were also satisfied with our new location, but there was a strong desire growing within them. They wanted a son who could carry on the family name. They both began to pray and ask God to fulfill that desire according to

His will. God chose to answer their prayers. Within a few short years of our move to the country, my parents announced that there would be a new addition to our family. This wonderful son, named after my father, would be the last sibling born into our family. We were now a family of seven, living in the beautiful mountains of West Virginia and surrounded by family.

Along with the many fun-filled outdoor experiences, I was also blessed with a wonderful spiritual heritage. My parents and grandparents all raised me to know Jesus Christ as Savior and Lord. Each of my grandfathers was a minister. One grandfather was a pastor, and the other was an evangelist who held revivals in a tent with sawdust floors. Additionally, each of my grandparents would sing to the glory of God. My first memories of singing solos to the Lord were in the tent revivals that my papa Taylor held. I still cherish the beautiful memories of being in the presence of God with them during many church services.

My teenage years were very much like my childhood years. By this time my dad had become a pastor, so we spent a great deal of time in church services. I always enjoyed our local youth group's Bible studies, nursing home visits, neighborhood tract distribution,

Christmas programs, and frequent trips to the local ice cream shop. From about the age of twelve, I was a committed participant and leader in the many revivals, vacation Bible schools, youth camps, and other church and ministry activities. I had developed a love for the Lord at a very young age, and that love continued to grow into my adult years.

Finally, in my early twenties, I married the man of my dreams. Travis was tall, dark, and handsome, as is commonly said. I met him when I was sixteen years old; my oldest sister married his brother. I was certain he was supposed to be my husband. However, the enemy fought to prevent our marriage for a long time. Through the grace of God and the prayers of many individuals, we miraculously became husband and wife after seven long years. Travis was also a believer in Jesus Christ, and he was a fantastic teacher of the Word of God. He could hold the attention of any congregation at length with his many visual aids and dramatizations of Bible stories.

Our first three years of marriage had the normal challenges of newlyweds, but they were otherwise wonderful. Easter Sunday of 1993 would prove very memorable for Travis and me—this was the day we announced that we were expecting our first child. We were so excited to start our family in our two-story rented home in the small town of Bluefield, West Virginia. About two weeks prior to Christmas of that year, we were blessed with a precious son who looked just like his daddy. Up to this point in my life, everything seemed to be a fairy tale with the happily ever after ending. Unfortunately, within the next year, my life would begin to unravel because of the hidden secrets that held me captive deep within my soul.

Chapter 2

The Unraveling

WITHIN SIX MONTHS OF our son's birth, we had moved into a different house. The move was to help us better accommodate the added expenses of a new baby. Life was pleasurable with our recent addition to the family; however, as any new parent knows, there are many stressors that arise with this tiny person who now consumes your life. The undivided attention that is required by an infant, the lack of sleep due to the nightly feedings, the evening colic, the extra laundry, and the unkempt house all became overwhelming. The external pressures were great, but the inside pressure was even greater.

There were dark, hidden wounds within me that no one knew about—and I intended to keep it that way. *Those are things of the past, they did not affect me, and no one needs to know,* I reasoned. *These are my wounds and my wrong choices,* I continued to argue. Daily there was an inward battle between my reasoning and God's liberating truth. Eventually I began to feel that I owed my husband complete honesty. I felt that he had given himself completely to me. I had only given him a portion of myself. I had given him the part that I wanted him to see. He was not allowed to see my bruised, bleeding, and broken heart. He was not allowed to see the fearful, insecure little girl. He did not need to know the shamed young lady. The image that he knew was the perfect wife, loving mother, and strong Christian woman—and I was content to let it be that way.

Eventually the inward suppression of the wounds began to affect my mind and emotions. I was tormented to the point that I became depressed. I did not want to believe that I, as a Christian, could possibly be suffering from depression. One day a Christian magazine from a well-trusted family ministry came in the mail. As I glanced through the pages, I saw an article titled "Christians and Depression." I immediately closed the magazine and went to hide it in the back of the drawer of my filing cabinet. I suppose I felt that if I ignored the problem, it would go away. I had always heard that

Christians could not suffer from depression. Hence, I deduced that if I had depression, I was not a Christian. I felt I had nowhere to turn for help.

I had also begun to be affected in many other ways. My sleep became disturbed. I would have tormenting nightmares almost nightly. I would awaken both myself and my husband as I screamed in terror. Furthermore, my body was afflicted by the turmoil in my mind and emotions. I started having headaches and dizzy spells for seemingly no reason. I would often feel as if I were going to black out. I would have to stop whatever I was doing and lie down. My husband, who was in the medical field, suggested that there must be an explanation for the symptoms. We began the search for answers.

First, I was scheduled to have an MRI done on my brain. This is a noninvasive medical test that takes images of the soft tissues of the body. I know that my next statement sounds absurd, but I was secretly hoping the doctors would find a tumor as the cause of my problems. I reasoned that if there was a physical cause, that would free me from the obligation of exposing my awful secrets. To my relief and dismay, the MRI reports came back normal. Nothing was found that could account for all my physical ailments.

After the MRI disclosed there were no medical problems in my brain, we set up an appointment with a greatly respected doctor at the local hospital where Travis worked. During the office visit, I had blood and urine tests done. Both came back normal. Soon the doctor came into the examining room and began to talk with me about the test results and my symptoms. He then explained his diagnosis and the preferred treatment. I will never forget his disheartening words.

"I believe that you are suffering from depression. What do you think?"

"Yes, I believe that is what is wrong," was my saddened response. Then he suggested a mild antidepressant pill and wrote out the prescription.

During this time in my life, I had no understanding of the power that exists in spoken words. I did not realize that, because I was made in the image and likeness of God, every word that I speak is creative.

> Then God said, "Let us make mankind in our image, in our likeness." (Genesis 1:26 NIV)

> Truly I tell you, if anyone says to this mountain, "Go, throw yourself into the

sea," and does not doubt in their heart but
believes that what they say will happen,
it will be done for them. (Mark 11:23–
24 NIV)

Bless the Lord, O you his angels, you
mighty ones who do his word, obeying
the voice of the word. (Psalm 103:20 ESV)

I was unaware that my words were allowing or
denying the enemy access to my life. If I speak positively
and in agreement with the Word of God, angels are
activated to carry out the words that I have spoken.
Likewise, demons, who are fallen angels, are also
activated by spoken words. Thus, if I speak negatively
and in opposition to the Word of God, demons are
released to bring about what I have just spoken.

When I walked out of the doctor's office that day,
I had three things: a diagnosis, a prescription, and an
open door for demonic spirits to attack me in an even
greater way.

Chapter 3

One Horrific Evening

I WILL NEVER FORGET THE awful evening of my diagnosis. As I left the doctor's office and drove home, there was a whirlwind of thoughts swirling around in my mind. I knew that my tormenting secrets were causing the inner turmoil and physical symptoms, also that the only way to stop the destruction was to bring the wreckage out into the open. Once I was back at home, I called my husband and shared the crushing diagnosis. While on the phone, I also mentioned that there were some other issues we needed to talk about when he got home.

As the hour of revelation drew closer, I became more nervous about telling my husband what had happened to me. How would he respond? Would he see me as dirty? Would he have a hard time dealing with what he was about to hear? Would it change his extreme love and respect for me? Would he walk away? Would he try to take our son from me? Would I, once again, be mistreated by another man? The voices in my head screamed loudly and clearly to keep me silent.

By mid-afternoon I had laid our infant son in his crib for a nap. Much to my surprise and God's plan, he was still asleep when my husband finally arrived at home. The door of the house opened, and in walked Travis. He immediately came to me, took me by the hand, and set me on his lap.

"I already know what happened," he said. "The Lord showed it to me on the way home. You are going to be okay. We will get through this together." His words gave me a sense of relief, and I began to cry. Because I felt his comfort and support, I began to tell him what I had been through. I disclosed, without graphic details and names, that I had been molested by three different men when I was a child. I also told him that I was not a virgin when we married. There had been another man, but it was a rape. He listened intently and continued to hold me while I carefully uncovered the hidden wounds deep within.

With the negative diagnosis and tragic news weighing

upon us, Travis suggested that the family take a drive out in the country. We could talk and ease our minds. The first part of the evening was somewhat relieving; however, as the evening progressed I became sick in a way I had never experienced before. I began having trouble breathing. It was as if I could not take in enough oxygen. I felt lightheaded and very nauseated. I began to tingle in my face and arms. My hands began to draw closed with cramps, and my jaws felt locked shut. I had chills and trembled all over. Travis encouraged me to slow down my breathing. He was praying for me and doing everything that he knew to do medically to assist me. Unfortunately, nothing seemed to help. Within the hour, we were in the emergency room of the hospital where he worked.

The evening continued to unfold with an even more intense situation. When we reached the hospital, I was in such a terrible physical condition that I could not even walk. Travis had to give our son to one of his fellow employees so that he could carry me into the hospital. Once I was in the emergency room, the medical staff began the routine procedure of evaluating my condition. My breathing was so labored that I began to feel as though I was going to die. With fear on my face and

Chapter 4
New Authority

THE NEXT MORNING WAS not as chaotic. However, it was just as memorable as the night before. I awoke at home, in my own bed, still fully clothed in what I had been wearing the previous evening. The house was totally quiet, which was not the norm since we had an infant son. I immediately called out for my husband. When he came into the bedroom, he explained that my sister and her husband had come to the hospital and taken our son to their house for the night. The medicine had sedated me, so Travis had carried me into the house and laid me down to sleep for the night.

The morning continued at a very slow pace. Along with breakfast, I took an antidepressant pill that the doctor had sent home with Travis. After I took a shower, I went to my parents' home to stay while he drove to the pharmacy to get my prescription filled. While at my parents' home, I began to feel the effects of the antidepressant pill I had taken earlier. I was sitting quietly in the living room chair, yet I was experiencing an out-of-body feeling. I could see everyone and hear what they were saying, but it seemed as though I had no control over my conversation or my own body. I felt as if I were outside my body, watching events take place.

When Travis returned with the prescription, he suggested that we go to the mall to spend a little time together. While in the mall, I began to experience a sense of paranoia. I started feeling as if everyone was looking at me. I began to think that everyone knew what I had been through and that they were looking at me in a demeaning way. I could feel fear trying to come upon me to cause another panic attack. However, the medication was preventing it from fully taking over my body. We soon decided to leave the mall and go pick up our son from my sister's house.

We took the short drive to my sister's house. It seemed like forever since I was anticipating being reunited with our son. I was so excited to see him and to be able to hold him once again; likewise, he was very happy to be with Mommy and Daddy. I remember standing outside in the driveway while trying to explain to my sister the details of the previous evening. It was at that moment that I also chose, with much shame and fear, to disclose to her the unfortunate occurrences that had put me in this state of depression. Travis and I spent a little time with my sister and her family. Then we started for home.

As we traveled the few miles back to our home, I began to cry about the uncertainty we faced. Travis reached over and gently took my hand. He began reassuring me that I was going to be okay and that we would work through each of the issues at hand. I desperately told him I did not want him to leave me the next morning.

The dreadful questions had already begun to bombard my mind with great force: "What if it happens again? What if I cannot make a call for help? What if I am holding our son and I drop him because of my hands cramping?" Travis explained that he had to go to work and that I would be okay because Jesus would be with me throughout the day. He then suggested that we pray.

Travis began to pray lovingly over me as we continued the drive home. I joined him in the prayer, and suddenly something happened to me. I heard the Holy Spirit within me say, "You are a child of God; you do not have to live like this for the rest of your life." Suddenly a boldness came over me that I had not previously known. I then began to touch each area of my body that had been affected with these new strange symptoms. I then began to command each part—"Mind, you will not worry or fear! You will think on good things. Jaws, you will not be tight any longer! Mouth, be opened freely. Stomach, be calm now, in Jesus's name. Hands, be opened! You will function properly. Body, be calm! You will not tremble any longer. I am a child of God, and you have no place in my body. Depression and fear, leave now! I am free in Jesus's name."

By the time that I had finished taking authority over my body and the enemy, we had arrived home. After a few minutes of rejoicing over my newfound boldness and victory, Travis and I got out of the car and went into the house. He put our sleeping son to bed, and I went to get the antidepressant medication. I took the prescription bottle into the bathroom and flushed all the pills down the toilet. I then called my mother to describe what had happened and to declare my freedom from depression. The events that unfolded that evening would prove to be only the beginning of many steps to my wholeness.

Chapter 5

The Dream

W HEN WE WENT TO bed that night, I had the same
terrifying dream three times.

In the dream, my son and I were at home by ourselves.
It was broad daylight. He was playing on the living room
floor while I completed the daily tasks of a stay-at-
home mom. While walking through the living room,
I suddenly noticed a black car racing quickly through
the field that was across the road from our house. The
car appeared to be a 1940s model with many dents and
rust that had eaten through the body in various places.
I watched through the window as an older, scraggly lady
stepped out of the car. She was dressed in black, tattered
clothing. Her hair was gray and stringy, and her teeth
were rotten. I saw that she was carrying a black bag over
her shoulder; it appeared to be a bat bag that was used

for carrying baseball bats. I knew within my spirit that the bag contained her dangerous weapons. I sensed that she was the spirit of lust.

This spirit of lust quickly approached our house and tried to find a point of access. She was sneaking around to each of the windows to see if there was an opening. When she did not find an entrance, she came to the front door. The inside door was standing open, but the outside storm door was locked tightly. She grabbed the handle of the storm door and began to shake it violently.

Travis and I were suddenly awakened as I screamed in terror. He immediately began to rebuke the enemy and pray over me. Within just moments I had fallen back asleep; unfortunately, I had the same horrible dream and experience all over again. Finally, as the night progressed, I was once again harassed by the same dreadful dream a third time; but, the outcome was wondrously different.

When the spirit of lust tried to get into the house the final time, I began to cry out to God for directions about how to make this spirit go away. In that instant, she was at the front door and forcefully trying to get inside. My eyes were drawn to my Bible, which lay open on the coffee table. I quickly grabbed my Bible and went running for the door. I was holding my Bible, with both hands, straight out in front of me. Rapidly I ran through the storm door and slammed my Bible directly into the chest of the demonic spirit. Immediately and powerfully, the spirit vanished before my eyes.

When I awoke the third time, I had a strong sense of victory in my spirit. I knew that God had set me free from the tormenting spirit of lust. I also had learned a very important lesson. The Bible is the weapon we must use to receive victory over all demonic spirits. Jesus taught us this lesson during his time of temptation in the wilderness. Each time the Son of God was tempted by the devil, He quoted from the Word of God to defeat him.

> The devil said to him, "If you are the Son of God, tell this stone to become bread."
>
> Jesus answered, "It is written: 'Man shall not live on bread alone.'"
>
> The devil led him up to a high place and showed him in an instant all the kingdoms of the world.

And he said to him, "I will give you all their authority and splendor; it has been given to me, and I can give it to anyone I want to.

If you worship me, it will all be yours."

Jesus answered, "It is written: 'Worship the Lord your God and serve him only.'"

The devil led him to Jerusalem and had him stand on the highest point of the temple. "If you are the Son of God," he said, "throw yourself down from here.

For it is written: "'He will command his angels concerning you to guard you carefully;

They will lift you up in their hands, so that you will not strike your foot against a stone.'"

Jesus answered, "It is said: 'Do not put the Lord your God to the test.'"

When the devil had finished all this tempting, he left him until an opportune time.

Jesus returned to Galilee in the power of the Spirit. (Luke 4:3–13 NIV)

I had certainly experienced a great breakthrough on this memorable night. Yet there were still other hidden matters in my soul that would soon be addressed by the patient heavenly Father.

Chapter 6

The Complete Unveiling

A PPROXIMATELY FOUR YEARS HAD passed since the dream about winning the victory over the spirit of lust, and our lives had changed in many ways. By this point we had been blessed with another son, and we were expecting our first daughter. We had also spent two years pastoring a church that was about one hour away from our family. While we were pastoring, the Lord began to speak to both Travis and me about moving elsewhere to be youth pastors. The time for reappointment of the pastors soon came; however, Travis declined the offer to remain as pastor. We felt certain we were supposed to leave.

Weeks passed by, and there were no youth pastorate opportunities available to us. The church overseer then offered us the opportunity to pastor a different church.

We did accept the opening with much hesitation, but shortly thereafter, we knew that the choice was a definite mistake. Finally we decided that we must take the blind leap of faith. No appointment as pastor to a church meant that Travis would now be unemployed and that we would be without housing. Graciously, my parents allowed us to stay at their home until the Lord had opened the door for us to do youth pastoring.

On the outside, Travis and I were making many decisions about our future. On the inside, I had once again begun to struggle with a lie concerning my past. During the time of opposing struggles, the Lord began allowing us the privilege of doing revivals in different locations. One of those locations of ministry was in Indiana. The burden to silence the lie and expose the truth became greater while we were in Indiana. I squirmed within because I did not want my shameful mistake to be revealed. I was mortified that I had committed the forbidden sin. I was also terrified that my husband would leave me if he knew the truth about me.

"I should just leave things alone," I reasoned within. "This secret is not hurting anyone."

When the revival was over in Indiana, we set out for our long drive back to my parents' home in West

Virginia. This was before the days of the GPS to direct one's every turn. Surprisingly, by a providential wrong turn, we ended up on some very lonely back roads. These roads had many harvest fields and very few houses. Both of our toddler sons were asleep in the back seat, and there was no radio reception of any kind. I kept sensing that now was the time to tell the full truth; however, fear would continue to silence me.

Finally, after many miles, we spotted a small, lonely roadside store. As a pregnant mother in dire need of a restroom, I found this place a welcome sight. While in the cramped, dirty restroom, the mental battle raged greatly within my head. The devil was trying to convince me that Travis would put me out on the side of the road and leave me to die, along with our baby in the womb.

"You will never see your sons or your family again. You will be picked up by a stranger and killed," Satan yelled to me.

The Lord would then console me with His words: "I am with you. It will be okay. Your husband will not leave you. These are all lies. I want you to be totally free. Trust me."

I was so desperate for this freedom of which the heavenly Father was speaking that I was willing to take the risk of baring my soul.

After using the restroom, I rejoined my husband and sleeping toddlers in our van. Once we had returned to traveling the lonely back roads, I nervously began my discourse with my husband.

"I need to talk with you about something very important," I started. "Do you remember when I told you about the molestation and rape?"

"Yes," he replied.

"Well, it was not the full truth," I continued. "I did go through the molestations, but there was not a rape. I had not done much dating when he asked me out, so I was flattered to have a new boyfriend. Unfortunately, I was naïve and he was very persuasive with his words. Before I knew what happened we were sexually involved; I never wanted to have sex before marriage. Sadly, there was no way to undo the mistake. I am so sorry for the lie. I was so ashamed of myself for what I had done that I could not face the truth about me. I am so sorry for all the pain that I am inflicting upon you. Please forgive me."

Just as the Lord had promised me, Travis did not put me out on the side of the road. As expected, he was bombarded with many emotions toward the other person involved and toward me. He responded with silence, then questions, and finally avoidance for many days. After his time of processing the situation and talking with the Lord, Travis chose to accept me once again. I remember him expressing his regret over my unfortunate past and his forgiveness toward me. The words that followed his forgiveness are words I will always cherish.

"You were a Christian when I married you. The Bible says that Christianity makes us anew."

> Therefore, if any man be in Christ, he
> is a new creature: old things are passed
> away; behold, all things are become new.
> (2 Corinthians 5:17 KJV)

"The word *new* means to have never been used. You were a virgin on the day I married you, and you will always be my virgin."

Wow! How great is the love of our heavenly Father? And how wonderful to be the recipient of His love through another person! This expression and reception of the Father's love unlocked the door to my soul. It created access by which Jesus could get inside and begin the deep healing process. This new liberty was miraculous;

consequently, when the Lord began to deal with me on the next issue, it was easier to respond quickly.

After the earlier emergency room experience, I had also lied to my oldest sister about the same situation. Now the Lord wanted me to tell her the truth for two reasons. I would be released from the shame, and she could be released from bitterness toward the alleged offender. She and I were at a church convention together when the Lord told me to tell the truth to her. When the altar service was over, we went into a private room. There I disclosed the actuality of the situation and asked for her forgiveness. She expressed that she could understand the difficulty of unveiling my sin and that she absolutely forgave me. I walked out of that room totally free from that burden, and the future would bring a liberty that I had never known before.

Chapter 7

Open Door

URING THE ELEVEN MONTHS we lived with my parents, life had changed remarkably for us. We had been able to get out of debt, our relationship had become stronger, and we now had three children. It was during this time that the Lord began our transition toward the plan of ministry he had prepared for us. When our daughter was four months old, we finally walked through the open door. The Lord had given us the opportunity to be youth pastors at a church in North Carolina. It was challenging to leave our family and move four hours away with three children under the age of five. Thankfully, the church people were very welcoming to our family, and they immediately began to connect with our children. Our schedule became quite busy with the readjustments of the move, caring for our three children, and ministering to the youth of the church. We were excited about the connection that was taking place, yet it still seemed something was missing in our lives.

Within a few months of our arrival at the church, my heart developed a cry for more of God. The church people were wonderful, but I knew that there was more freedom than we were experiencing.

One day Travis came to me and said, "Honey, please be praying with me about where the Lord wants us in ministry." That seemed a strange request to make; we had just left our family and home state to follow the Lord. In that moment, I knew God was shifting us again. Travis and I began to pray for God's directions, and God began to make the necessary connections for the next move. After a short time had passed, we attended camp meeting services at a nearby church. It was during those few nights we realized we had found what we sought. There was freedom of worship, a flow of the Holy Spirit, and revelation of the Word. We had never encountered anything like it before this time.

Travis soon disclosed to me that only months earlier, the Lord had said to him, "I brought you here to take you elsewhere." We knew that God wanted more growth in us, which would require us to be at the other church. There was one detail that the Lord would need to work out on our behalf. Travis was a full-time youth pastor, so we were financially dependent upon the church where he was employed. If we were going to pursue God's direction, God would have to provide a new source of income. We began to pray about the situation, and miraculously God did provide. One day while we were at home, a man from the new church came to offer Travis a job at his business. Travis accepted the offer, and within a few short weeks, our family would be attending the new church. However, God had a plan to show his love through us one more time during our last service as youth pastors.

The youth group was assigned to facilitate a Sunday evening service once a month. The teenagers were responsible for the worship, playing the instruments, performing skits, and other activities. Often I would lead the praise team and congregation in worship, and then Travis would minister the Word of God.

As I began leading the worship, the atmosphere intensified with the presence of the Holy Spirit. It was then that the Lord prompted me to disclose publicly that I had been through molestation and that God was truly a healer. I told the group that God's healing power could help us to overcome any obstacle in our past. When I began to affirm God's healing power, the healer came into the sanctuary to minister to and help each one who was present. During the continuance of worship and prayer, there were mothers and grandmothers who confessed to me that they also had been molested or raped. I was privileged to lay hands on them and pray for God to heal the deep wounds of their emotions. Little did I know the depth of the freedom that God had planned for me, and I did not yet know that He would use me to bring healing to many other wounded souls. As the evening service ended, God led us into the next chapter of our lives.

Chapter 8

New Freedom

IT WAS WITH GREAT excitement that we attended our first service at the new church. The worship was so strong and free. We would often spend thirty minutes to an hour focusing on Jesus and receiving the love of our heavenly Father. The pastor would then minister through the Word of God. It would come forth with such revelation that it was difficult to take notes on everything that the Father was speaking through the pastor. Altar services were powerful. Many souls were saved, and people received help from God in a variety of ways. My husband and I were like sponges, soaking in every new experience with the Lord.

Within a short time of our arrival at the new church, the Lord connected me to a lady who would become my spiritual mentor and be instrumental in my complete healing. She had suffered many unfortunate wounds in her past, yet she was free through God's healing grace. We spent many hours on the phone while she graciously imparted to me the many lessons that she had learned through her healing process. I would then apply the new knowledge, and gradually the chains began to break off my own life.

During this time of healing, the Lord used another tool to aid in my freedom. I was watching inspirational television early one morning, and I saw an interview with Beth Moore. She is a Bible teacher who has authored many books and Bible studies. She was talking about her book, *Breaking Free*.

A voice within my spirit said, "You need that book." At the end of the show, the director offered the book for "a gift of any amount." During this season of our lives, we were homeschooling our three children; we were a one-income family. Our finances were so tight that I could not afford to send even a small monetary gift to receive the book.

Later that morning a friend from church gave me a phone call. I began to tell her about the show I had seen and the details of the book. I did not mention anything about purchasing the book. A few hours later, I received another call from the same friend. She asked if she could come to visit with me on the following day. I expressed my excitement and offered her lunch with the children and me.

On the following morning, I prepared the house and the lunch for her anticipated arrival. When she showed up at our home, she brought unexpected gifts to my family and me. There were many groceries, frozen home-grown vegetables, and *Breaking Free*. I was excited about her generosity but even more thrilled about the book. It was overwhelming to realize that God had moved upon her heart to purchase the book for me. I knew that this book would be a key to more freedom.

I was anxious about reading the book. By the end of the day, I had already finished the first two chapters.

The Lord then spoke to me and said, "Go back to the beginning of the book and start again. This time around, let the book read you. I will set you free in many ways."

The next morning, I started on a new journey with the Holy Spirit and *Breaking Free* as my companions. As I read through the book, the Holy Spirit would show me where I needed to be freed. I would then begin to pray and follow His instructions. Gradually the wounds were healed, and the chains began to fall away. It took more than a year's time for the healing process through which the Holy Spirit led me. What a transformation took place in me! The heavenly Father wanted me totally free, so there were still more steps that I would go through to get there.

Moore, Beth; *Breaking Free,* First edition, 2000.

Chapter 9

Public Revealing

A FTER I HAD GONE through the healing process, the Lord began to open doors for me to minister freedom to others. One of those opportunities came when I was invited to speak at the youth camp that our church hosted. Upon receiving the request, I began to pray about what the Holy Spirit would have me share each evening. He started speaking to me about sharing my personal testimony. My husband was hesitant about me doing so because he did not want others to lose their respect for me. The Holy Spirit directed me as I responded to my husband's concerns.

"Who I am today is not dependent upon my past or what others think of me." Travis then gave me his blessing to share all that the Lord was speaking to me.

After much prayer and preparation, the time for

youth camp finally arrived. I inquired of the Lord daily about which message he wanted me to deliver that night. On one of those mornings, the Lord said, "Tonight is the night." I was okay with that until, later in the afternoon, many of the leaders from our church came to hear the evening message. I then confided in one of my friends about what was going on inside me.

"I am not telling this in front of all of them. I will choose another message from the ones I have prepared." She told me that I must do as the Lord had instructed, and that she would be praying for me. As I spent some time alone with the Lord, he explained his purpose, "You must tell it all so that you and many others can be set free."

When the evening service approached, the building was packed with the teens, the camp staff, and many church leaders. I stood before the crowd and fully disclosed the wounds of my childhood, my mistakes, and the lies I had used to cover each of them. I told how God had so carefully healed each wound, and how mercifully he had forgiven each mistake. I explained that God was not angry with anyone and that his love is unconditional. The Lord then instructed me to ask the adults to participate in the altar call. He wanted those who had been delivered from issues with which teenagers may struggle to come forward. I then asked them to pass the microphone and simply state the issues from which the Lord had delivered them. I felt that the teenagers would more freely expose their struggles to people who had already won victory in the same areas.

What happened next was totally unexpected. The first person began to give details of her own wounds and failures. She then passed the microphone, and the next adult did the same thing.

I remember thinking, "This is not what I had intended." I wanted to explain that they did not have to give any details about their past mistakes.

The Lord said to me, "Be still. I am setting others free." As the microphone was passed down the line, many deep wounds were exposed. Molestation, abortion, rape, drug addiction, alcohol abuse, and enslavement to pornography were all disclosed. Some adults already had the victory in an area, and they prayed over the teens. Other adults, who had very deep wounds, received healing that night. Husbands and wives held one another and sobbed as God ministered to them. Children forgave their parents for the mistakes of their past. Granddaughters brought healing as they embraced their wounded grandmothers. Marriages were restored in the presence of God. God had turned the packed room into a hospital. How amazing are His ways!

I must admit that exposing the dark secrets was not easy; however, God was with me that night. He gave me grace to be completely honest, and I experienced a new type of liberty that I had not known. The Bible describes this liberty in Proverbs 29 (NIV): "Fear of man will prove to be a snare, but whoever trusts in the Lord is kept safe."

It is far more important that we trust the Lord's direction instead of worrying about what people think about us. On this miraculous evening, I was set free from the fear of man. I was no longer concerned with what others thought of me; on the contrary, I realized that many people would like to be free of their pasts.

Because of what I had been through, I learned to be compassionate, forgiving, and nonjudgmental. I then had a revelation that even the wounds and mistakes of my past could be used to help bring healing to others. The Bible instructs us on this kind of healing and comfort.

Praise be to the God and Father of our Lord Jesus Christ, the Father of compassion and the God of all comfort, who comforts us in all our troubles, so that we can comfort those in any trouble with the comfort we ourselves receive from God. (2 Corinthians 1:3–4, NIV)

I also realized that I do not have to be perfect for the Lord to use me. There was still another related inner issue from which I would be released.

Chapter 10

No More Regret

"**W**HY DID THAT HAPPEN to me?"

"I would not wish this type of abuse on my worst enemy."

"Life would have been so different had I not gone through that."

"My innocence and childhood were stolen from me."

"I cannot believe that I made that choice."

"I knew better."

"I will never get over it."

"I can never forgive myself."

"If I could go back to that moment, I would surely do things differently."

"If only I could erase that day from my life."

Do these statements sound familiar to you? They have been on replay multiple times in my own mind, and I have also heard them from other women as they shared their unfortunate stories.

All people can recall incidents they regret. For me, of course, the incidents of molestation and premarital sex were the two events I always wished had not happened. I spent many days imagining what life would have been like without the fear, nightmares, shame, and guilt. I tried to figure out why I was the unfortunate victim, although I never wanted anyone else to take my place. I would ponder the wrong choices and determine what I should have done differently. Sadly, no matter how many times I mulled it over, I could not change anything. Each incident was irreversible and carried definite consequences, tormenting me for many years.

Early one morning, as I prepared to go to my job, I began to weep. My husband questioned me about why I was crying.

I explained, "I know that God has forgiven me for the sin of premarital sex. Why can I not forgive myself? It has been many years, yet I still live with this regret. Will I ever get over my past?"

I then went into the bathroom to finish getting ready for work.

It was then that Holy Spirit spoke to me. "Go look up the word *regret*," He said.

I immediately went to get a dictionary. The definition is *to mourn the loss or death of; to be keenly sorry for.* The prefix *re-* means *again*, according to *Webster's Seventh New Collegiate Dictionary.* I quickly realized that I was grieving the loss of my innocence and my virginity, but how was I to get over it? How could I stop the grief from overtaking me?

Later in the day, I began to search the Bible to see what it said about grief. I learned that grieving (mourning) was never meant to be a lifestyle. Mourning should only last for a brief season, then it should come to an end, as written in the Bible.

> To every thing there is a season, and a time to every purpose under the heaven: ... A time to weep, and a time to laugh; a time to mourn, and a time to dance. (Ecclesiastes 3:1–4 KJV)

In Psalm 30:5 (NIV), we are also reminded that pain is temporary: "Weeping may stay for the night, but rejoicing comes in the morning."

Satan, our enemy, wants us to grieve for the rest of our lives over the misfortunes that we have suffered or the bad choices that we have made. God, our loving Father, wants us to repent, be healed, and walk in the joy that He has given to us.

I also learned that, in biblical times, people often put on sackcloth and bowed down in ashes. This custom is described in 2 Samuel 3:31, Genesis 37:34, Esther 3 and 4, and Jonah 3:5–8. People wore sackcloth to show grief over losing someone who was dearly loved. When a person wore sackcloth, smeared ashes on the face, and sat in ashes, it symbolized repentance of sin. Satan wants to keep us in sackcloth and ashes. He wants us to grieve over our losses for a lifetime. He also tries to oppress us with shame so that we feel the need to be continually bowed over in repentance.

I do believe we should repent of our sins; however, there is a difference between conviction and condemnation. Conviction occurs when the Holy Spirit shows one that he has sinned and encourages him to repent and be changed. Condemnation occurs when Satan continually reminds people of their sins and forces them to revisit their shame. Conviction is beneficial; on the other hand, condemnation is detrimental. In Romans, Jesus' viewpoint of condemnation is clearly stated.

There is therefore now no condemnation
to them which are in Christ Jesus, who
walk not after the flesh, but after the
Spirit. (Romans 8:1 KJV)

With the above revelation, I received a new freedom
that I had never before experienced. I realized that
Satan had been bullying me for many years with the
shame of my past. I finally understood that, since I was
in Christ, there was no more condemnation. At that
moment, I refused to live another day with shame and
condemnation. The following song was birthed out of
my newfound liberty.

I refuse to cry any longer.

I refuse to sit in the ashes.

I refuse to hang my head in shame.

For I know that your blood has cleansed me.

You have washed me whiter than snow.

So I receive rejoicing in your name.

Jesus is His name.

Jesus, restorer of my soul.

You have healed me, cleansed me, and made me whole.

(Repeat three times.)

Jesus is His name.

(Repeat three times.)

And I will never be the same.

Why do some people go free from their pasts while others do not? Freedom is a choice that each person must make. To receive true freedom, we must first come into a relationship with Jesus Christ as our personal Savior. Then, as we spend time with him, we begin to realize all that he paid for at Calvary. Once an individual receives a revelation of deliverance through Jesus Christ, it is up to that person to receive the gift that He has paid for through His blood. Finally, we must refuse to bow to the lies and condemnation of the enemy. In John 8:36

(KJV), Saint John states the situation clearly: "If the Son therefore shall make you free, ye shall be free indeed."

It is now time to let go of the past and to move into the freedom that Christ has prepared for you.

Your Healing
and Future

Chapter 11

The Questions

Q UITE OFTEN, WHEN YOU go through something as painful as a molestation or rape, there are many questions that haunt you.

"Did I do something to cause the perpetrator to be attracted to me? Why did my parents leave me in this situation? Why did I not speak up earlier so that the nightmare would stop? Why did this loving God not step in and stop it all?"

These are just a few of the questions that you may have struggled with during the horror of abuse. I will do my best to explain the answers that brought peace to me and aided in my healing.

"Did I do something to cause my perpetrator to be attracted to me?"

When you have been through molestation, rape, or any other type of abuse, it is not your fault. An abuser is bound by sin and perverted in his or her mind. This person's behavior has been distorted and is not normal. Often the offender may have either been corrupted through abuse, an enslavement to pornography, or even a drug addiction. Whatever the case may be, you are not guilty. You did nothing to encourage the wrong behavior. Perpetrators are driven by the evil within to find someone with whom to fulfill their selfish, sick desire. Satan wants to put guilt and shame on you that rightfully belong to the perpetrator. He works tirelessly to keep you bound in the pain of your past. God does not want you to be in pain.

> "For I know the plans I have for you," declares the Lord, "plans to prosper you and not to harm you, plans to give you hope and a future." (Jeremiah 29:11 NIV)

God has so many wonderful days ahead for you. He wants to set you free to enjoy a bright future and assist others in their freedom. Your freedom is your choice. You were an innocent victim, but you can choose to be an intentional victor.

"Why did my parents leave me in this situation?"

This was the hardest question for me. They are Christian parents who have always sought to protect me. They were always very cautious about whom we could visit or with whom we could spend the night.

"Why would they leave me with someone who would hurt me so badly? How could they not have known that I would be abused?" I puzzled in my mind.

As I grew into adulthood and realized what loving parents I truly have, I found my answers. They are only human; they could not have known that I would become a victim of abuse. I am convinced that if they had known, they would have done everything within their power to prevent the exploitation from happening.

Unfortunately, you may not have been raised in a loving family where you always felt protected. Your parents may have lived in a selfish way that placed you in danger on a continual basis. Worse yet, your parent might have been the abuser. I certainly cannot identify with such a damaging scenario. I also do not intend to belittle the trauma that you faced; however, it is a regrettable fact that individuals parent from who they are on the inside. If a person is internally wounded, it is possible that they will hurt others either emotionally or physically. Whatever your case may be, please know that God is well able to help you to forgive your parents.

"Why did I not speak up earlier so that the nightmare would stop?"

The previous question taunted me for many years. I believe that one of the reasons that I did not speak up is because, no matter how old I became, I was still a frightened little girl inside. I was always fearful that if I told on them, they would come back and hurt me even more or hurt someone else I loved.

Guilt was another emotion that caused me not to speak out about the abuse. When I was told, "This is *our* little secret. Don't tell anyone, or *we* could get in trouble," I became very confused and began to question my participation in the horrible act. If the preceding deception is not combated with the truth, you will begin to internalize ownership for what has happened. Satan will try to convince you that you deserve punishment for your behavior. He will then try to keep you silent even longer, extending your season of captivity.

The final argument for not speaking of the abuse is the nature of the topic. Sexuality is usually a very uneasy topic of discussion for adults, and it is certainly an even more uncomfortable issue for a child. An abused child who has been thrust into an adult problem is surely not capable of handling the situation. I believe that many individuals suppress the dark secret until they have matured enough in their reasoning to sort out the details of the abuse. They have finally come to a mental age where they feel somewhat secure talking about the abuse. For me, twenty-six was the guarded age when I chose to speak of the multiple molestations and my own failures.

I encourage anyone who has been victimized not to postpone the uncovering of the wounds. The longer you put it off, the more the emotional wounds will fester and affect your life. My safe place was my husband; yours may be a spouse, friend, pastor, or even a counselor. Even though I disclosed the deep wounds of my heart, I still struggled with the same negative emotions from time to time. In my spirit, I knew that there was more healing to come. Patiently and compassionately, our loving heavenly Father would eventually take away all of the pain and damaged emotions.

Finally, **"Why did this loving God not step in and stop it all?**

> Then God said, 'Let Us make man in
> Our image, according to Our likeness; let

them have dominion over the fish of the
sea, over the birds of the air, and over the
cattle, over all the earth and over every
creeping thing that creeps on the earth."
(Genesis 1:26 NKJV)

God has dominion over all creation; however, he
appointed mankind to rule over the earth. Whatever takes
place on the earth is man's responsibility, not God's fault.

In Matthew 6:10 (NKJV), Jesus instructed his
disciples to pray, "Your kingdom come. Your will be
done, on earth as it is in heaven."

God wants everything in the earth to be just like
it is in heaven. I believe that, through prayer, we can
avert some negative occurrences. Regrettably, we are
not always aware of the planned attacks of the enemy,
nor are we in control of the actions of all people. People
have free will to make their own choices; unfortunately,
their choices have consequences that will sometimes
affect others. Also, there is still sin in the earth, and
where there is sin, there is pain. It may not be possible
to live a life that is totally free of trouble, but God can
bring healing to each bruised heart and redeem each
damaged life.

Chapter 12

Confession for Healing

THE TRAUMA OF ABUSE is often very difficult to discuss. It is also a great challenge to address the shame, painful memories, and extreme emotions. You generally suppress the shameful ordeal for a great length of time. You may be of the belief that the pain will just go away; unfortunately, that is not at all the case in this situation. Abuse of any type causes very deep emotional wounds. Simply covering the wounds will not heal them. This is like putting a stick-on bandage over a wound that requires surgery.

Jesus Christ is known as the great physician because he alone has the power to heal the body, spirit, and soul. Jesus speaks of himself as the healer of the heart.

> The Spirit of the Lord is upon Me …
> because He has anointed Me, He has
> sent Me to heal the brokenhearted. (Luke
> 4:18 KJV)

Jesus is the only one who can heal your heart, but you must first be willing to uncover the wound in His presence.

Through my own healing, I learned that one key to my restoration was talking to someone that I trusted. I shared with my husband, my sisters, and close friends. As I look back upon this process, I realize that, with each confession, it became easier to talk about. I also noticed that Satan would try to use intimidation to make me uneasy about what others thought of me. I now understand that his tactic was an attempt to keep me in an emotional prison. I learned that, once I had begun to expose the secrets, they began to lose their power over me. Once you choose to bring to light the dark secrets, then you become a candidate for the healing power of Jesus Christ. In James 5:16, we are instructed to "confess your sins to each other and pray for each other so that you may be healed."

This scripture speaks of confessing sins to one

another for healing. The definition of *healed* is "to cure, heal; to make whole; to free from errors and sins; to bring about one's salvation." (Strong's G2390) I have also found that we can apply this same scripture for deliverance from emotional wounds. When we confess wounds that are caused by another's sins and pray for one another, then we are also healed. The internal healing of emotional wounds can begin a positive transformation that will affect each area of your life.

Once I had begun to expose the wounds, I also gained an understanding of the feelings with which I was struggling. I learned that the shame and guilt did not belong to me; they belonged to the perpetrator. Satan tries to weigh you down with shame and guilt until you walk around with your face to the ground. If he can keep you bound in shame, you will believe that your value is that of the dirt upon which you look daily.

In Psalm 3:3 (NLT), the psalmist declares, "But you, Lord, are a shield around me, my glory, the One who lifts my head high."

Satan does not want your head to be lifted high— then that you will see the light of a brand-new day. Declare this aloud.

I am innocent. I refuse to bear the guilt
and shame of my abuser. Jesus, thank you
for removing the guilt and shame. Thank
you, heavenly Father, for being the lifter
of my head. I see new light, and I have a
bright future in Jesus Christ.

When you speak these words in the name of Jesus,
you will sense that the chains that once bound you are
now gone. You are now free to continue the healing
process.

When you have suffered abuse, you always carry a
great deal of pain in your emotions. The pain, unlike
the shame and guilt, is authentic and does belong to
the victim. When you start talking about the abuse,
the pain will begin to surface. This can often be an
overwhelming task; consequently, you may be tempted
to stop talking about the abuse and continue to suppress
the pain. Suppressing the pain seems to be an easy way
out; however, hidden pain is a poison that will cause
internal destruction, relationship problems, and health
issues. In Isaiah 53:4 (NIV), the prophet states that
Jesus has taken away our pain: "Surely he took up our
pain and bore our suffering."

Jesus will not forcefully take the pain from you; on the contrary, you must release it to Him. When you willingly offer your pain to Him, He will remove it and mend your heart. Pain from abuse usually comes in many layers. God knows what you can handle at any given time. He will unveil each memory or pain at the right time. If He unveils it, you are ready to face it and release it. Trust Him as He takes you through the healing process. It is so amazing to release your wounds to the King of kings and finally be free from the pain of abuse!

Chapter 13

Forgiveness Is the Key

I WILL ALWAYS REMEMBER THE grotesquely vivid dream that the Holy Spirit gave to me during my healing process.

I was outside of my body, and I was standing at a distance to view my front side. I saw that I was standing in a cruciform position with hands extended left and right. I watched as my chest and abdomen were split vertically and opened completely. Both sides rolled back like a scroll being unrolled. I then observed a large maggot inside my chest cavity that was eating and squirming; it was full of life. I asked God, "What does this mean?"

He then explained, "Maggots feed on that which is dead and decaying. You have many wounds; thus, you are dying inside. The maggot is large because it has been feeding on your pain and bitterness for years."

Suddenly I witnessed a great explosion inside my chest that ignited a fire. The fire began to spread throughout my entire body and burn into my head, toes, and fingertips. When the fire had fully finished burning, my body quickly sealed shut. I noticed instantly that the outside of my body was glowing. It had the appearance of a brilliantly shining silver coating.

When I awoke from the dream, I realized that I had deep inner healing that needed to be done. I was also aware that the restoration would only happen if I cooperated with the Holy Spirit. I would like to tell you that I was eager to start forgiving my abusers, but I was very resistant to releasing them because I did not feel that they deserved forgiveness.

The Holy Spirit began to speak to my heart about studying the crucifixion of Jesus and following his example as one who forgives. There are three specific aspects of forgiveness that can be found as Jesus hung on the cross. Firstly, Jesus chose to forgive. He had been betrayed, mocked, whipped, punched, spat upon, crowned with thorns, and crucified naked. Still, he was determined to let it go. In Luke 23:34 (NIV), Jesus said,

"Father, forgive them, for they do not know what they are doing."

Forgive means *to refrain from enforcing a punishment or sentence.*

While Jesus was on the earth, he was fully God and fully man. He had the power to execute judgment upon his abusers; he chose to forgive them. Jesus won an immeasurable victory for all of mankind with his choice to forgive. When we choose to forgive our perpetrators, we win a great victory for ourselves and others. Our wholeness allows us to build healthier relationships with others.

Practicing forgiveness does not indicate that you must never go to court and have the perpetrator punished by the law of the land. I do feel that there should be a penalty for crime. If you choose not to get the law involved, know that God will avenge you. Sometimes the individual will suffer something tragic; other times, God will defeat the enemy by giving you a tremendous spiritual victory. He will transform you into such a different person that there is no residue of abuse anywhere in your life.

If you choose or have chosen to go to the law, be aware that many times the consequence does not fit the crime that was done to you. You may go through the trial, get a strong sentence, and feel completely justified; the reverse could also happen. Your perpetrator may get no or little punishment, causing you to feel even more violated by the jury and the law. Whether or not you feel vindicated by the sentence that is given to your abuser, it is still crucial that you forgive that person. If you choose not to forgive others, you will become bitter. Hebrews 12:15 (NLT) confirms the danger of bitterness, "Watch out that no poisonous root of bitterness grows up to trouble you, corrupting many."

The Bible indicates that bitterness acts as a poison that eats away at your emotions year after year. If bitterness is left unchecked for any length of time, it can damage your health and contaminate your relationships.

Secondly, each of us is responsible for Jesus's death. He still forgave us so we could come into right standing with God. It is our sin that put Him on the cross. In 2 Corinthians 5:21 (NLT), we read, "For God made Christ, who never sinned, to be the offering for our sin, so that we could be made right with God through Christ."

Jesus forgave you and me for our sins long before we were ever born. He knew that the only way for us to be made right was through his forgiveness. When we choose to forgive others, it allows them the opportunity to experience the love of Christ. It is His love and grace that will invite them to come into right standing with God. In Ephesians 4:32 (KJV), it is written, "And be ye kind (mild) one to another, tenderhearted (merciful), forgiving one another, even as God for Christ's sake hath forgiven you."

When we realize all that Christ has purged from us, it makes forgiving others a much easier task. We are then able to look at our violators through the eyes of compassion and see their need for mercy. Also, we recognize that God forgave us for Christ's sake. *Christ* means *anointed*. (Strong's, G5547) Anointing is the power or effectiveness that comes from the Holy Spirit in the life of a believer. If we choose not to forgive others, it hinders the effectiveness of the Holy Spirit's work in our lives and our effectiveness in helping others. When we choose to forgive, we become instruments through which the Holy Spirit can flow to assist others.

Thirdly, Jesus also mentioned that his abusers and murderers did not know what they were doing. He was not indicating that they had no control over their actions, but they did not know that he was the Messiah and that they were being used by Satan. Your abusers do not understand that you are created in the image of God and that they are violating the heavenly Father as they mistreat one of his own. They also cannot possibly understand how much damage that they are causing. Even if they wanted to apologize and ask for your forgiveness, there is no way that they can compensate you for the pain that they have put you through.

In Ephesians, we can read an explanation of how we are to live.

> Imitate God, therefore, in everything you do, because you are his dear children. Live a life filled with love, following the example of Christ. (Ephesians 5:1–2 NLT)

Once I had made the choice to forgive, I became free in my soul in a way unknown in the past. The mental peace was amazing! I was no longer envisioning what bad things should happen to my abusers to avenge myself of the wrongdoing. I have chosen to allow God to handle retribution, as recommended in Romans.

> Do not take revenge, my dear friends, but leave room for God's wrath, for it is

written: 'It is mine to avenge; I will repay,'
says the Lord. (Romans 12:19 NIV)

I realize that forgiving your abuser sounds impossible, but it can be very easy. If you have chosen to follow Christ, he will give you the grace to do so. When you are sincere about releasing those who have harmed you, pray this simple prayer in the name of Jesus.

Father, I choose to forgive_____ for the abuse that he/she did to me. I give up my right to avenge myself, and I trust that you will avenge me. I repent for the sin of bitterness, and I ask that you take all bitterness out of me. I release _____ from my grasp of bitterness. Let your cleansing waters flow through me and purify my soul.

Chapter 14
Defining Soul Ties

GOD IS MADE UP of three parts: the Father, the Son, and the Holy Spirit. Man is created in the image and likeness of God; therefore, man is a three-part being. We are a spirit, we have a soul, and we live in a body. The spirit is the innermost part and instantly becomes perfect when we accept Jesus Christ as our personal Savior. The soul is the middle part that includes the mind, will, passions, and emotions. The body is the outermost part of our being and is physical in nature. It is the soul that I want us to investigate more deeply.

The soul is the place where we develop attachments. Emotional attachments, both positive and negative, are known as *soul ties*. We will first look at the positive soul ties, which are also called godly soul ties. God has ordained a variety of relationships that are to be blessings in our lives—marriage, family, extended family, friends, neighbors, coworkers, and brothers and sisters in Christ. The Bible addresses each of these soul ties, but I want us to take a closer look at two of them: marriage and friendship.

In Genesis, the bond of marriage is described as a very strong union.

> And Adam said, This is now bone of my bones, and flesh of my flesh: she shall be called Woman, because she was taken out of Man. Therefore shall a man leave his father and his mother, and shall cleave unto his wife: and they shall be one flesh. (Genesis 2:23–24 KJV)

When a husband and wife take the vow of marriage, an extreme soul tie is formed. The soul tie becomes stronger over time, especially when they have intercourse. As they grow together, they are literally becoming one flesh. Since marriage causes the couple to become one flesh, divorce is always harmful because there is an extreme tearing of the soul that only God can mend.

Friendship is another bond that develops soul ties. In 1 Samuel 18:1 is an account of a godly friendship between two young men.

> After David had finished talking with Saul, he met Jonathan, the king's son. There was an immediate bond between them, for Jonathan loved David. (1 Samuel 18:1 NLT)

This scripture indicates that Jonathan immediately knew that he and David had a kindred spirit and that there would be an enduring friendship. The King James version states that "Jonathan loved him as his own soul." This bond was manifested in three different ways as the years passed and their friendship grew stronger. First, Jonathan was supposed to be heir to the throne after his father, King Saul, was deceased. Jonathan was willing to give up the throne so his friend David could become king, thus fulfilling the plan of God (1 Samuel 20:31). Second, Jonathan protected David when King Saul was plotting to kill him (1 Samuel 19:1–3). Third, after David had become the king of Israel and Jonathan had died, David learned that Jonathan had a crippled son named Mephibosheth. David quickly moved

Mephibosheth into the palace, gave him land that had previously belonged to Saul's family, and even assigned servants to take care of the land for him (2 Samuel 9). Godly soul ties between friends can be lifelong bonds.

Marriage and friendship are examples of two godly soul ties. Next we will look at ungodly soul ties and how to deal with them.

Chapter 15

Ungodly Soul Ties

S OUL TIES CAN BE developed in many ways. The soul
tie of marriage is formed by taking a vow; thus,
it is a fact that all other vows, oaths, or promises of
commitment can form a soul tie. A soul tie can also be
developed by an obsession with a person such as a movie
star, performer, or band. Strong negative emotions
toward someone can also cause an ungodly soul tie.
Finally, the strongest soul tie that can be established
comes through any relationship that includes sexual
contact of any sort. This includes marriage, affairs,
premarital sex, party sex, homosexuality, and even
molestation or rape. In 1 Corinthians 6:18, we are
warned against sexual sins.

> Flee from sexual immorality. All other sins a person commits are outside the body, but whoever sins sexually, sins against their own body. (1 Corinthians 6:18 NIV)

All ungodly soul ties are damaging; however, the soul tie from sexual sins can be the most destructive to an individual because it is a deeper bond.

An ungodly soul tie forms an invisible connection between two people that allows unwelcomed influence in your life. Here are a few evidences that an ungodly soul tie may exist.

- Your mind is in turmoil a great deal of the time.
- You have problems making decisions that are beneficial for yourself.
- You continue to be drawn to bad habits or addictions, although you really do not want to participate in them.
- You have a continual replay in your mind of negative words spoken to or about you.
- You keep getting into abusive relationships, although you desperately want to be loved.
- You continue to be pulled back into a friendship or relationship that is harmful to you.

- You have moved on or even developed a different relationship, yet you cannot seem to get that other person out of your mind.
- You judge people based upon previous incidents or relationships.
- You always feel angry or defensive.
- You live with fear, paranoia, and depression.
- You have nightmares about abuse that happened in your past.
- You have recurring dreams about people from your past.
- You feel controlled by someone from your past, even though that person is already deceased.

I had many ungodly soul ties when my husband and I got married. However, he had no clue about the turbulence within me. I cried often for no reason. I suffered from panic attacks, paranoia, and depression. I had nightmares on a regular basis; I would wake up screaming in terror. I always dreamed of someone trying to rape me. No matter how much we talked and prayed about the issues, I still had the same struggles.

Finally I learned about ungodly soul ties and how to break them. When I applied this revelation, my life began to transform. The shame and guilt went away. I no longer struggled with depression, paranoia, and the abuse of my past. My mind became free to think more clearly. The bad memories no longer tormented me, and the nightmares stopped. The Holy Spirit had severed all ungodly soul ties and healed my mind and soul by the blood of Jesus. There was no more negativity flowing into my soul from my past. Wow, what freedom I had received!

Chapter 16

Hidden Soul Tie Revealed

FREEDOM FROM NEGATIVE SOUL ties continued for many years without the tormenting nightmares. Then I suddenly had a dream that included one of my abusers. The dream is as follows.

My family of six people was living in a small apartment. One of my sisters and her family were staying there for a visit. It was very crowded with a total of ten people there for the weekend. There was another apartment that was attached to the back of my apartment; they were connected by a walkway that was made of treated lumber. One of my abusers was living in the rear apartment. I had made homemade soup for dinner. My husband suggested I take a bowl of soup to my abuser. I then said, "No, I am not going to do it. My sister can do it."

When I woke up from the dream, I felt a staggering hatred toward my abuser. It was then that I realized I had reconstructed a negative soul tie with my abuser. I had recently learned that he had also harmed someone else; consequently, I became angry and bitter with him. I had forgiven him for what he had done to me, but I found it very difficult to forgive him for abusing the much younger victim.

The Lord began to show me, through the dream, that the bitterness would affect me, my immediate family, and others. I also realized that my bitterness was restricting God's increase and blessings in my life. The dream and the Word of God challenged me to forgive and break the newly formed ungodly soul tie. It would be somewhat easy to do the above acts; however, the next request was very difficult. My heavenly Father asked me to write a letter to this perpetrator, tell him that I had forgiven him for everything, and invite him to come to know Christ as his personal Savior.

Forgive him? Yes, I could do that. Offer Christ to him? No! I did not want him to be in heaven with me. He did not deserve it, not after everyone that he had harmed. Then the Holy Spirit chastised me through a familiar scripture, Romans 3:23 (KJV)—"For all have sinned, and come short of the glory of God."

He also reminded me that the Father loves us all unconditionally despite the nature of our sins. In Psalm 51:1, David writes of this unconditional love of the Father after he has sinned with Bathsheba.

> Have mercy on me, O God, because of your unfailing love. Because of your great compassion, blot out the stain of my sins. (Psalm 51:1 NLT)

God is love, and the measure of His love is not dependent upon the nature of our sin.

While I was getting ready for work that morning, the Lord gave me instructions to share my story and the dream with my tenth-grade Bible class. He also brought a song, "Forgiveness," by Matthew West, to my mind. I went to the Christian school where I was employed and began to prepare mentally for the afternoon Bible class. When class time finally came around, I began to disclose my story and the details of my morning. I *did not* tell the students about God telling me to write the letter. During my time of sharing, one of my students raised his hand.

I called him by name and asked, "Do you have something that you need to say?"

His response both shocked me and made me cry even harder. "Mrs. White, I feel like the Lord wants you to write a letter to your abuser and let him know that you forgive him."

Wow, what a confirmation! God sure has unique ways of speaking to us.

Upon sharing my story in class that day, I had full intentions of writing the letter, but something strange happened. Every time I started to write it, fear would overwhelm me. I feared that my abuser would come back and hurt me again. The heavenly Father assured me that I would not be harmed by sending the letter. He also reminded me that He had extended grace to all mankind even though we did not deserve it. He was asking that I extend grace to my perpetrator and allow him the chance to know Jesus.

All of us deserve to spend eternity in hell. However, through Jesus Christ, God has given us the opportunity to spend eternity in heaven. There is another clear truth in James 2:10 that puts everyone on a level playing field where sin is concerned: "For whoever keeps the whole law but fails in one point has become guilty of all of it." (James 2:10 ESV)

The sin of my offender was no greater than my own sin. How could I not give the same grace that had been given to me?

I finally submitted to what the Father was asking and wrote the letter. I told my abuser that I forgave him for his misdeeds to myself and others. I extended a sincere invitation for him to surrender his heart and life to Jesus Christ. I then repented of my bitterness and broke the ungodly soul tie that had formed between us. The results are that I have had no more dreams of him since. Now I do pray that he will receive the unconditional love of our heavenly Father and receive Jesus as his Savior. I would be thrilled to see his life transformed and see him in heaven one day.

Chapter 17

Breaking Ungodly Soul Ties

B REAKING AN UNGODLY SOUL tie is an easy process. Here are some simple steps to follow to receive freedom. First, you must be sincere in wanting to disconnect completely from the individual. Each victim is earnest about being free from the abuser; however, there are other situations to address. If you are currently stuck in a relationship that is not good for you and cannot seem to break away, ask God for the strength to get out of the bondage. God will help those who want help, but He will not force His freedom upon anyone. If you are willfully staying connected to an individual despite the warning signs, I pray that you will have a change of heart and come out of the dilemma. Thankfully, I have also witnessed God's miraculous power work in this kind of situation as God's people prayed. There is hope for you, but you must cooperate with God.

Second, you must be willing to repent of any sin that is involved with the soul tie. If you willfully participated in the addiction or relationship, repent for making wrong choices. When a soul tie is formed by abuse, there are many negative emotions that take root in a person's heart. We must then repent for harboring anger, bitterness, fear, and other negative emotions in our hearts and choose to forgive so we can be released.

Third, the heavenly Father may require something extra of you so that you can be completely free. Be sensitive to the Holy Spirit and do exactly what He requests of you. Complete obedience to the Holy Spirit is where you will find freedom from the past. He asked me to write a letter. Although it was a difficult request, I am certain that I would not be totally free had I not obeyed his request.

Fourth, when you pray, insert the name of each person with whom you wish to break a soul tie. Here is a sample prayer to use. However, I encourage you to follow the specific leads of the Holy Spirit. You may pray this prayer as often as necessary. When I first received the revelation of breaking ungodly soul ties, I had many soul ties from the past that needed to be broken. Now that I know to guard my heart and make wiser choices, I have fewer ungodly soul ties that need to be dealt with. God is so faithful to set his children free!

Heavenly Father, I come to you with a sincere heart. It is my desire to break the ungodly soul tie that I have with (person's name). I repent of my participation in the sin of (name the sin) with this individual. I repent of the negative emotions of (specify these emotions) that I have carried with me through the years.

I choose to forgive (individual) for (sin or abuse). I will no longer seek to get revenge. I release them now and forever. Because I have chosen to forgive them, I am also released.

I say that the blood of Jesus has forgiven me of this sin and cleansed my soul. I receive the healing power of Jesus Christ and say that all wounds related to this soul tie are healed by the stripes of Jesus.

I declare that the ungodly soul tie between us is now broken in Jesus's name. I am totally free from this soul tie so I can now move into the bright future that God has planned for me.

Chapter 18

Share Your Freedom

WHY DID I FEEL that it was necessary for me to tell my story? I spent many years in bondage, all the while wishing to be free. I was hurting deep within, yet no one was aware. I was fearful and harassed with nightmares, yet no one understood why I was tormented by the devil. I was engulfed in shame, yet I hid it well behind my strong, energetic personality. I became tired of the mental battle that I fought on a regular basis. I very much wanted to be free, so one day I chose to accept the unconditional love of the heavenly Father. Once I had accepted His love and healing, I became free and whole.

As I began sharing my story with individuals and small groups, I learned how widespread the problem of sexual abuse really is. No matter where I spoke, someone always shared the secret of their own trauma. Many came from adults, even grandparents, who had never told anyone. Since I had learned that exposing the dark secret was the first step to the healing process, I became even more determined to tell my story of God's healing power. The liberty that I had experienced was so intense that I wanted all hurting people to go free.

After you have received your complete healing, I also encourage you to share your story with others who may be secretly suffering. In 2 Corinthians, we learn about our responsibility to comfort others.

> He comforts us in all our troubles so that we can comfort others. When they are troubled, we will be able to give them the same comfort God has given us. (2 Corinthians 1:4 NLT)

Your healing is not something that should be kept a secret. Do not worry what others may think about you or your past; you are loved by God. Jesus wants you to share your story so that He may be glorified and others can go free. There is no wound too deep to be healed, and there is no sin too dark to be cleansed. God is love, and it is His perfect delight to heal and cleanse every individual.

In Romans 5:8 (NLT), we read, "But God showed his great love for us by sending Christ to die for us while we were still sinners."

Go now and share your story so that others may go free!

Printed in the United States
By Bookmasters